Curlilocks and the Sleepy Giant

TANGLED
PRESS

For Ben, Riley and Babe.
We play the way we practice.
YK

Summary: Curlilocks and her bestie, Nelson are going to play their cello and violin with Auntie Lizzie. There's a restless giant in their way. Will Curlilocks and Nelson be able to get the giant back to sleep so they can pass?

ISBN 978-0-9910272-9-3

Library of Congress Control Number 2018902418
Printed and bound in USA

Tangled Press
13359 N Hwy 183 Suite 526
Austin, Texas 78750
TangledPress.com

TANGLED
— PRESS —

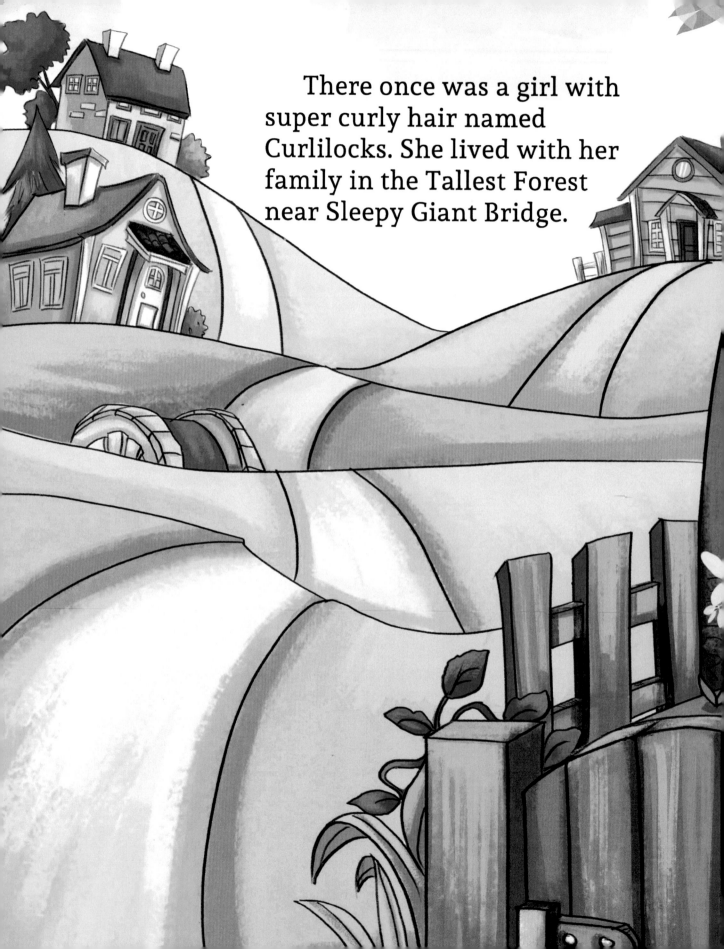

There once was a girl with super curly hair named Curlilocks. She lived with her family in the Tallest Forest near Sleepy Giant Bridge.

Monday was Jam Day. Curlilocks and her best friend, Nelson, were going to Auntie Lizzie's house. The two friends had been taking music lessons from Auntie Lizzie for months. They were ready for their first Jam Day. Curlilocks, Nelson and Auntie Lizzie were going to jam. They would play their instruments together.

Curlilocks and Nelson had practiced for 100 consecutive days. Curlilocks played the cello. Nelson played the violin. Auntie Lizzie played lots of instruments.

Curlilocks quickly put her breakfast plate away when she heard Nelson knock.

She nestled her cello into her red wagon, gave Dad a kiss and rushed out the door.

Dad called after them, "Mind the Sleepy Giant. And remember, practice makes progress."

The two friends strolled into the forest with their instruments. Curlilocks pulled her cello in a wagon and Nelson carried his violin.

Near a redwood sapling, the friends stopped. They spied a charm of hummingbirds. The birds hovered in the air as they drank nectar from a fire bush flower.

Nelson wondered, "How do they keep their wings up and strong?"

"I don't know," said Curlilocks. "I think it takes lots of practice."

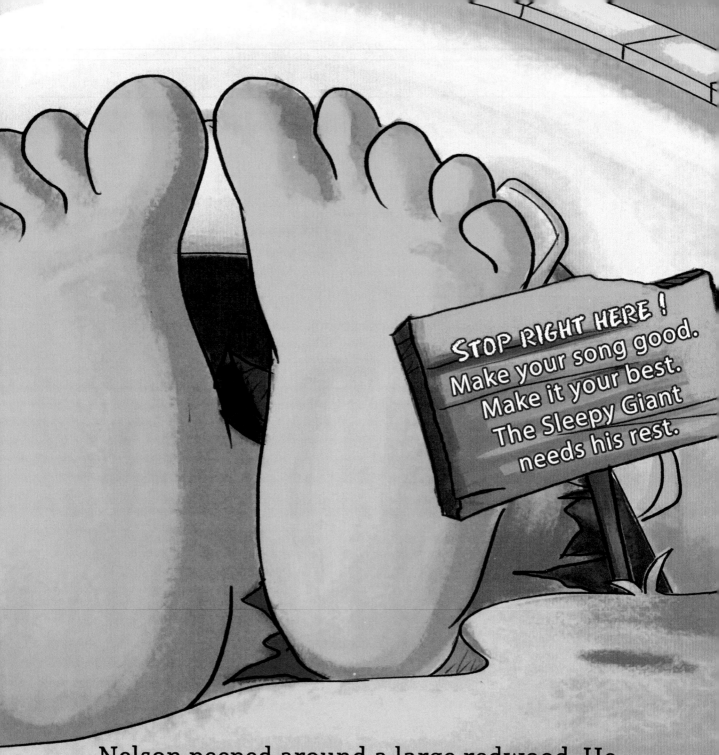

Nelson peeped around a large redwood. He
saw the Sleepy Giant's toes tapping under the
bridge. "We should hurry. The Sleepy Giant needs
to be fast asleep so we can cross the bridge."

The friends walked to the foot of the bridge and read the Sleepy Giant's sign. "Stop right here! Make your song good. Make it your best. The Sleepy Giant needs his rest."

"The Sleepy Giant is wide awake. What should we play?" Curlilocks asked Nelson. "Lullabies make me sleepy," said Nelson. "Excellent choice," said Curlilocks.

They took out their instruments and began a duet. The lullaby was soft and relaxing. The giant's feet slowly stopped tapping and he began to snore. "My arms are exhausted," said Nelson. "Mine too," said Curlilocks.

Suddenly, the Sleepy Giant's legs stuck straight out and he said, "Do-Re-Mi Rest. I hear the sound of your progress."

Curlilocks sighed. "We should start over, but my arms are still tired." Just then, two hummingbirds flew by and whispered, "Practice is the secret of keeping your wings up." "Thank you," said Curlilocks and Nelson.

Curlilocks sat down to play again on a large green rock. The Sleepy Giant was beginning to snore when, suddenly, Curlilocks fell off her seat.

The almost sleeping giant sat up and said, "Do-Re-Mi Rest. I hear the sound of your progress."

Curlilocks and Nelson looked and saw the rock was actually a giant tortoise. "I'm sorry. I thought your shell was a cozy rock," said Curlilocks. The tortoise blinked slowly and said, "It's quite okay my dears. Keep trying, your way is near."

The tortoise continued home and Curlilocks dusted herself off. "Let's try again," said Nelson.

The two friends began to play again. The giant's snores were getting louder and louder.

Suddenly, there was a "**bong-pop-plop**."
A string on Nelson's violin had snapped.

The giant sat up again and said, "Do-Re-Mi Rest. I hear the sound of your progress." "What should we do? Auntie Lizzie is waiting and the Sleepy Giant is still not asleep."

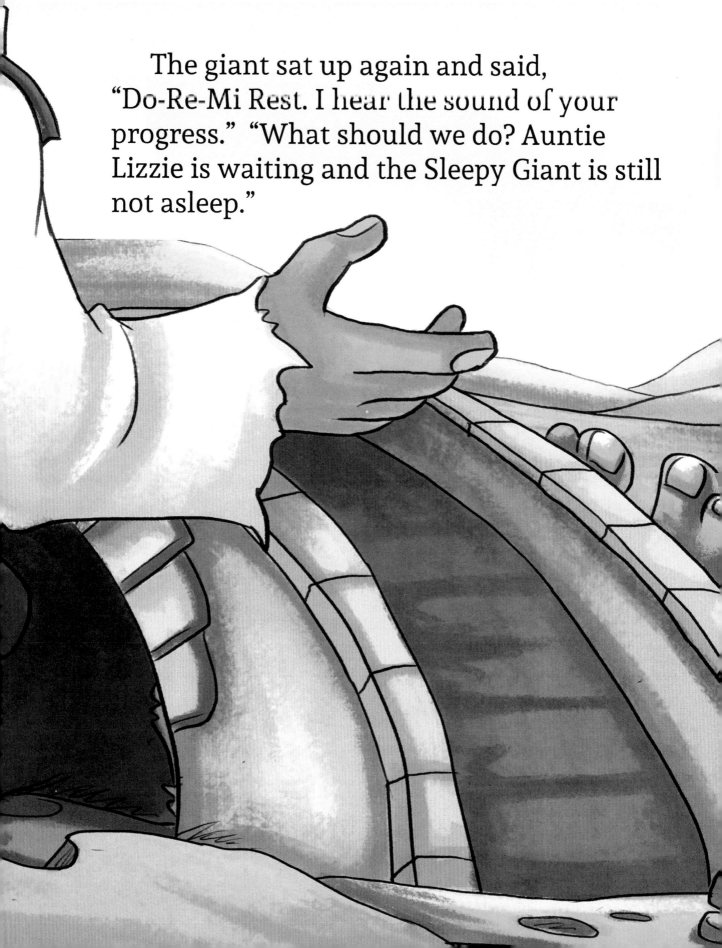

They needed to solve this problem.
Curlilocks quickly tugged the ribbon from her
super curly hair.

The friends pulled a strand of thread from the ribbon and fixed the violin.

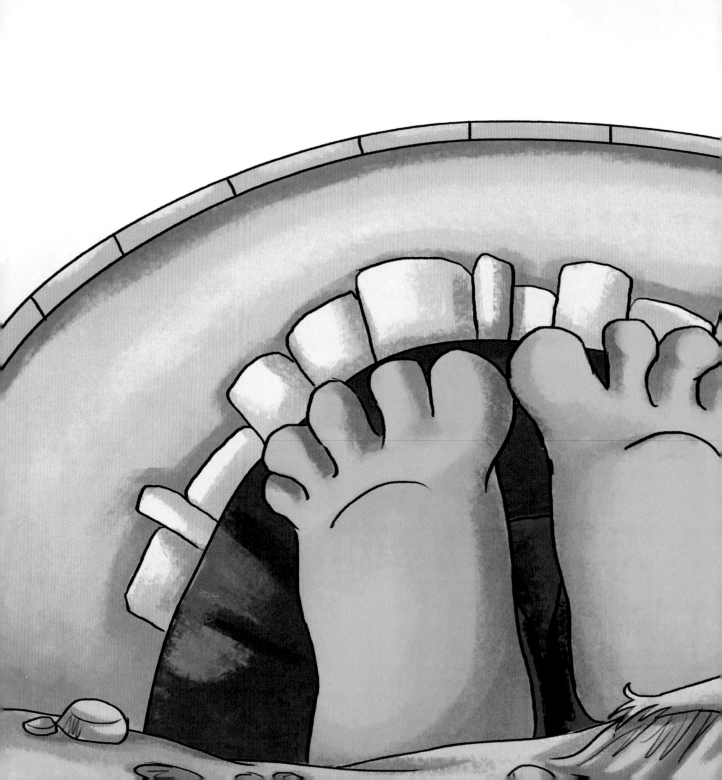

They began to play again and soon the Sleepy Giant was fast asleep. He was snoring loudly and deeply.

Curlilocks and Nelson leaped across the bridge.

Auntie Lizzie greeted them with peppermint tea, apple slices, and sweet potato pie. They each played their instruments and had a stupendous Jam session.

SLEEPY GIANT WORD LIST

Consecutive- in a row, one after the other
Sapling- a young tree

Charm of hummingbirds-
a group of hummingbirds

Duet- a performance by two people

Stupendous-
causing amazement

Visit us at www.TangledPress.com

89353051R00022

Made in the USA
San Bernardino, CA
23 September 2018